EYE CAN'T BELIEVE IT
INCREDIBLE OPTICAL ILLUSIONS

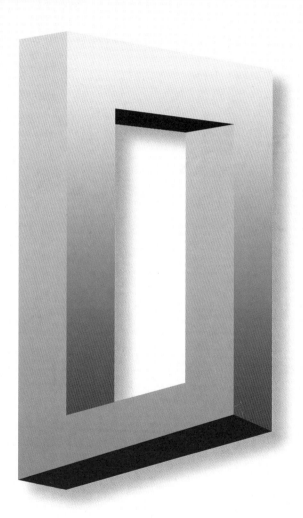

Reader's
Digest

The Reader's Digest Association, Inc.
Pleasantville, New York

A Reader's Digest Book

ISBN 0-7621-0675-1

Written by Bob Woods
Editor: Chip Lovitt
Art Director: Karen Viola
Project Manager/Designer: Joseph Matera
Illustrators: Joseph Matera — Cover, pages 1, 4 thru 24, 26 thru 37, 40, 42,
50, 51, 60 thru 93. Lindy Burnett — pages 41, 44, and 45, and art for the
thaumatropes and phenakistoscopes. Robin Brickman — pages 25, 43, 48,
and 49. Stereograms on pages 56 thru 59 created by Gary W. Priester.

EYE CAN'T BELIEVE IT

INCREDIBLE OPTICAL ILLUSIONS

Seeing Isn't Always Believing

Why the two don't always go together

Welcome to the wonderful, whimsical, and above all, fascinating world of optical illusions. Scientific principles might explain how such visual trickery works, but all you really need to know is that it does work. And that it's eye-popping, head-scratching, crowd-pleasing fun you simply can't resist.

Try to explain impossible objects. See stationary images move. Look at one picture as it reveals another. Discover hidden images and messages. Make sure what you're reading is really what's written. You won't believe your eyes...and you shouldn't!

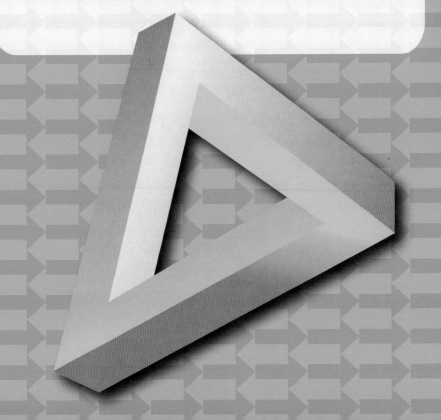

Eyes Versus Brain

*T*hings aren't always as they appear to be...or are they? That's the puzzling reality of optical illusions, which are simply tricks that our eyes and brain play on each other. We think we see something that's not there—or don't see something that's in plain sight.

An amazing thing about optical illusions is that there are so many different ways to visually fool ourselves. For example, look closely at the cleverly drawn image above and see if there's more than first meets the eye. Or gaze at the grid of various-size squares on the opposite page that make a flat checkerboard appear three-dimensional. Then look at the goblet to the right. What else do you see?

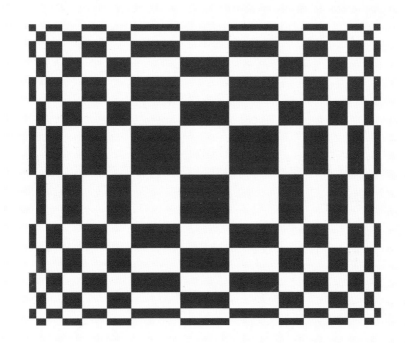

Special Eyes

While we ponder the wonders of optical illusions, it's important to understand how our amazing eyes work. Each one has a protective outer layer, the cornea. Light enters through a small hole called the pupil, which is a dark spot in the middle of the iris, a muscular disk that expands and contracts the pupil. Behind this is the lens, which focuses the light onto the retina. The retina, a screen at the back of the eye, then leads to the optic nerve, which carries the light to the brain, where the visual messages are processed.

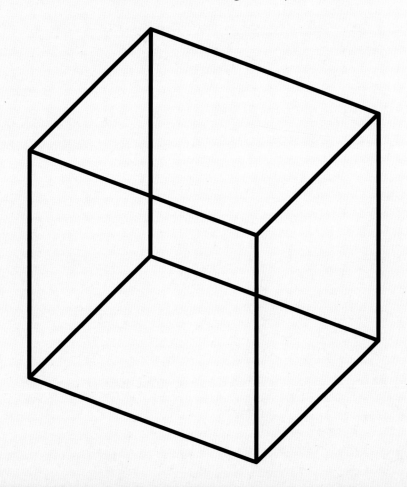

Points of Views

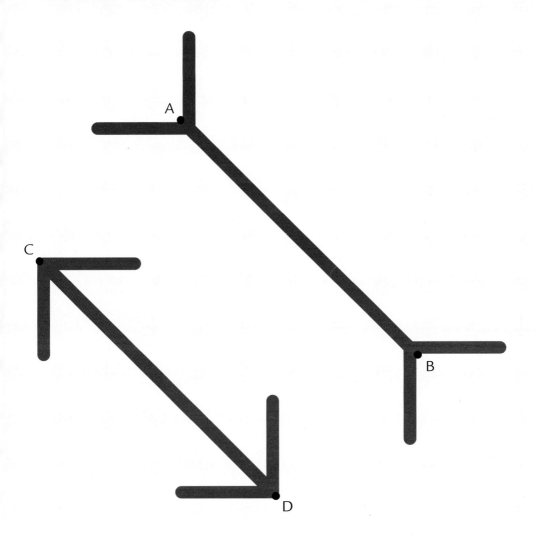

The 3-D cube to the left is a classic example of eye-brain shenanigans. Depending on how you choose to look at it, your brain "sees" a box that opens from different angles. Equally puzzling are the images above. Which line is longer? Our brains say A to B, because the ends open outward versus the inward ends on C to D. Measure the lines from black dot to black dot, and you'll see they are equal.

Focus Pocus

Sometimes, depending on where our eyes focus, we see different things in the same image. In this classic illusion, you can shift back and forth from seeing a frog or a horse by holding the book either vertically or horizontally.

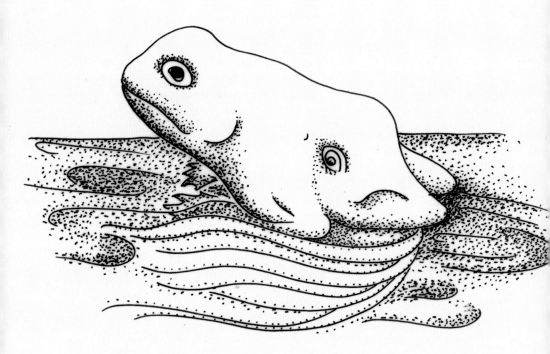

Ambiguous Figures

Ambiguous figures are those that are not exactly clear or definitive. They can be interpreted two different ways, depending on how you look at them. Here are two timeless examples. Does the top drawing show an open book or the outside covers? Is the wheel of cheese missing a slice, or is there an upturned wedge in front of it?

Impossible Objects

What's really real...or not

You look at an image one way and think you see something. But then you look at it another way and see something quite different. You stare at a geometric drawing or shape long enough and suddenly realize that there's no way it could actually be built. These illusions are called "impossible objects," because it really isn't possible to figure them out, much less construct them. What is possible, though, is to keep trying to make sense of these vexing visuals. Good luck!

Four Goes into Two Equals Three

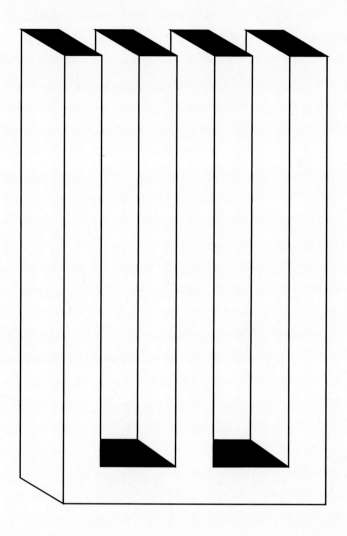

When you look at this figure from the top, it first appears to be a series of four rectangular columns. But follow it to the bottom, and it turns into a pair of open slots. Look again, though, and you'll also see a three-pronged fork pointing up. How can that be?

Frame of Mind Game

So what on earth is this? One moment you see a rectangular frame. Yet as you look longer, and trace the shape, there's no way it could possibly exist as a real object. It is equally challenging to figure out whether it faces up and to the left or down and to the right.

Tri, Tri Again

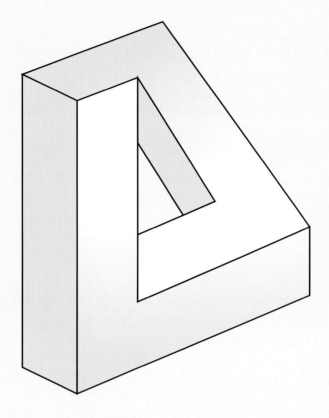

This perplexing optical illusion is one of several variations of an impossible object called a tribar. The "simple" form is a triangular shape that simply can't be explained, no matter how much you try. This truncated tribar plays tricks with your sense of perspective. Regardless of which angle you focus on, it's impossible to sensibly connect the pieces.

A Tribar with a Twist

Here's another type of perplexing tribar. Note how the perspective seems to shift and the triangle's sides seem to be twisted. As you ponder it, imagine trying to build such a structure using children's blocks. You can only imagine it since it would be impossible.

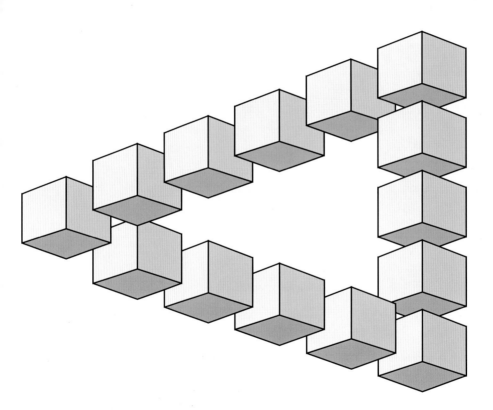

See for Your Shelf

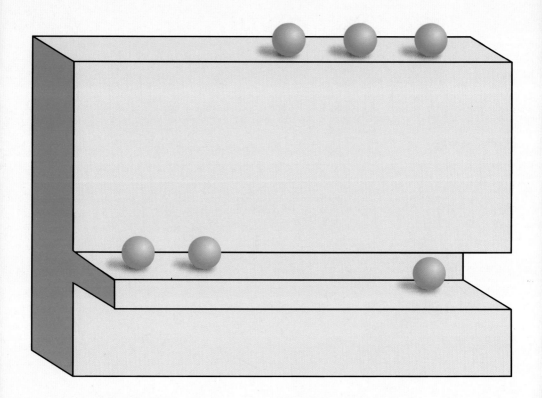

Viewed from the left side, this appears to be a shelf affixed to a beam. Start from the right, though, and it's a grooved beam with an upper and lower shelf. Now, focusing on the lower three balls, dart your eyes back and forth.

Up the Down Staircase

Step right up and try to find the highest point on this impossible staircase. Give up? Then see if you can locate the lowest point. Stare at these stairs long enough and you might find yourself climbing the walls!

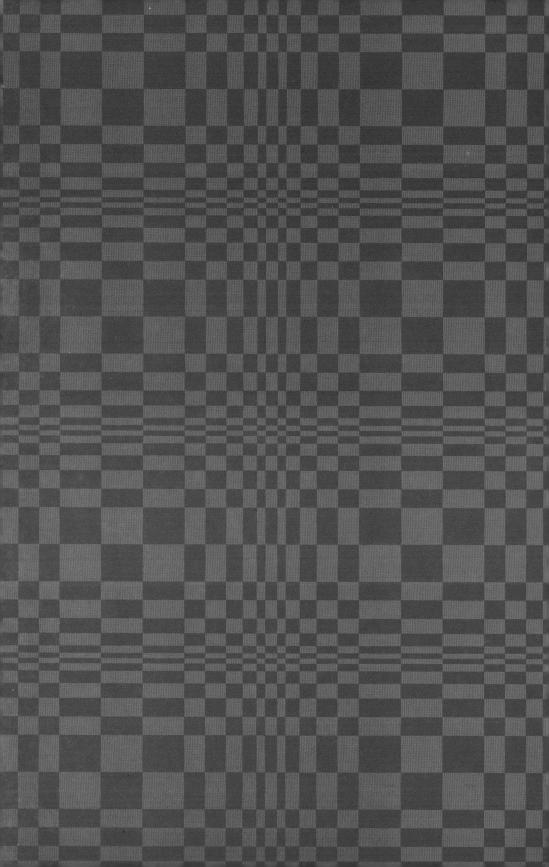

Classic Illusions

Timeless optical teasers

The visual trickery of optical illusions has been popular since the early 1800s, in one form or another. The French reveled in finding hidden images of Napoleon in illustrations of flowers. Artists such as M. C. Escher loved to tease viewers with impossible images and perplexing perspectives. Op (for "optical") Art became all the rage during the 1960s. More recently, computer graphics have unleashed another dimension of ocular oddities. What follows is a trove of traditional trickery.

Color Confusion

YELLOW BLUE

ORANGE BLACK

RED GREEN

PURPLE YELLOW

RED ORANGE

GREEN BLACK

BLUE RED

PURPLE GREEN

BLUE ORANGE

You might think it's easy enough to read this chart, but here's the trick: Say the color, not the word. You'll be surprised at how twisted your tongue becomes. Your eye may recognize the color, but your brain sees the word first. In this case, the mind is quicker than the eye!

Dots Weird!

Stare at this pattern of different-size dots for a few minutes and you'll see a rippling, revolving effect. Just roll with it, though. Logic says stationary images can't move, but don't believe it.

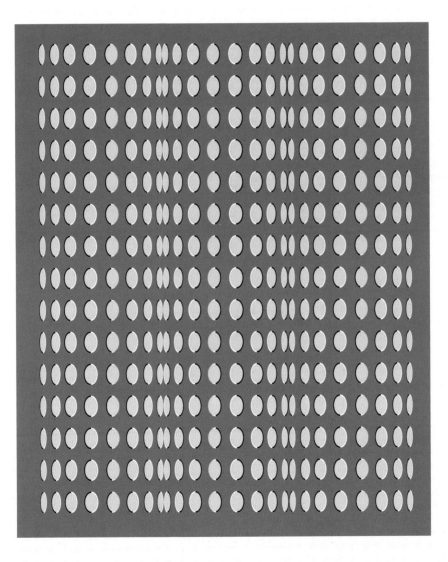

See Spot...or Not

In this flowerlike design, your eyes may see gray or white spots where the black lines intersect. You may also see light gray concentric rings. Of course, they're just illusions. There really are no spots or rings. This effect results from the way your eyes react to the interaction of light and dark.

Who Nose What It Is?

If you see the protrusion on the left side of this image as a nose, it's a profile of a man. See it as an arm, however, and the image morphs into the rear view of an Eskimo peering into a dark cave.

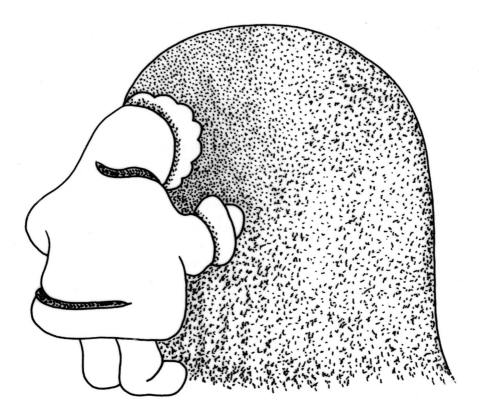

What's the Point?

Are the arrows in this image red or light blue? It all depends on how you look at it, but the answer is both.

Going Up...and Down

Here's a variation on the previous illusion. Are there green arrows pointing up? Or are there yellow arrows pointing down? The beauty of this puzzling picture is that you're right, either way.

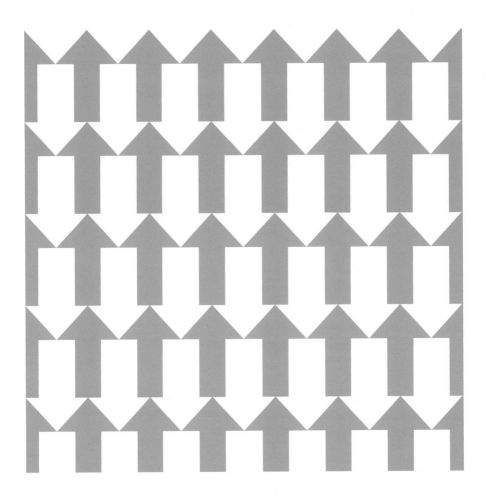

Eye Exam

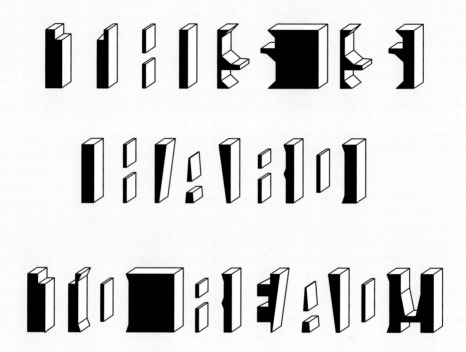

Close-up, this image appears to be a meaningless bunch of shaded blocks. But squint at it from an arm's length away, and you'll see a hidden message.

Answer on page 94

Pants on Fire

To tell the truth, the profile of this man isn't all that it first appears to be. Turn it 90 degrees counterclockwise, and you won't believe what's revealed.

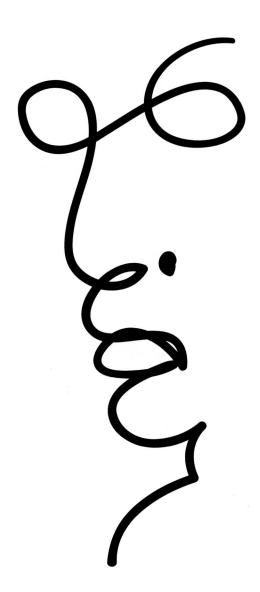

Spooky Spirals

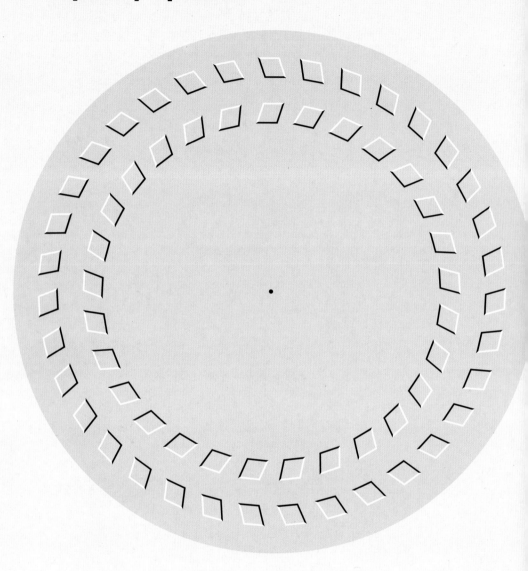

Hold this image still and it's just a series of boxes. But stare at the black dot and slowly move it toward you, and then away from your eyes. The boxes magically spin—in different directions.

Different Point of View

At first glance, this looks like one of those ubiquitous bar codes we see everywhere. But when you hold it at eye level, tilt it forward at about a 45-degree angle, close one eye, and look again, you'll break the code. Can you read the hidden words?

Answer on page 94

Diamond Vision

Gaze upon this maze of intersecting lines for a few moments, and you'll see the diamonds—a small one inside a larger one. Depending on your focus, the small one rises above or recedes into the larger one. Either way, it's a rich experience.

This Is Not a Test

Since the 1920s, doctors have given patients a psychological exam, called a Rorschach test, where they look at pictures of ink blots and tell what they see. In this non-scientific variation, our eyes take in the ink blots, but our brains fill in the rest of the picture. What do you see here?

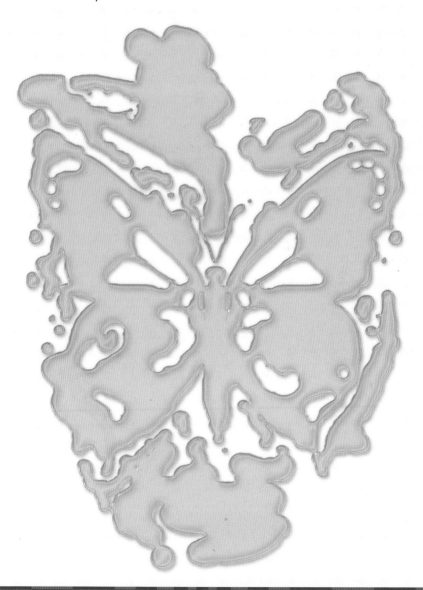

Now You See Dot, Now You Don't

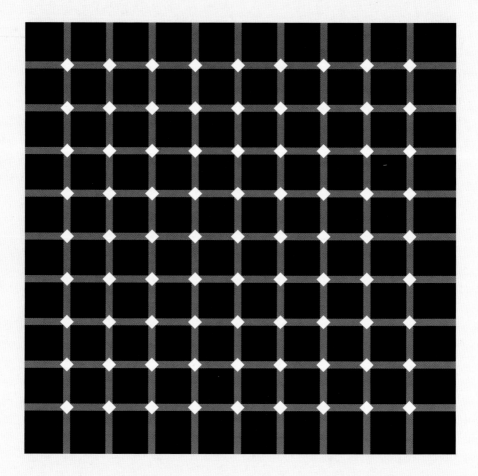

As your eyes wander around this so-called "scintillating grid," you'll notice black dots appear—and disappear—at the intersections of the gray lines. The dots come and go due to our eyes' reaction to the tight black-and-white pattern. Distance does play a role: If you look at the grid from either very close up or far away, the illusion doesn't work.

Connect-the-Dots

Up close, this appears to be no more than a grid of black and white dots. Look at it from several feet away, however, and an image will be revealed. This visual principle—that tiny black and white dots can form a picture—is the same one at work in black and white newspaper and magazine photos. (Use a magnifying glass on a newspaper photo and see for yourself.)

Mind-Bender

This is a great example of how sometimes your eyes and brain can't quite get it together. When you look at the squares against the zigzag background, the lines seem crooked. In fact, they're perfectly straight. It's a scientific principle called the Zollner effect. When straight lines are viewed against a background of curved or zigzagging lines, they seem to bend. When you tilt the image down slightly and away from you, you'll see the lines are perfectly straight.

Zollner Strikes Again

Here's another version of the Zollner effect. This time, though, it's a background of concentric circles that does the trick. Again, tilt the image down and away from you and you'll be seeing straight again.

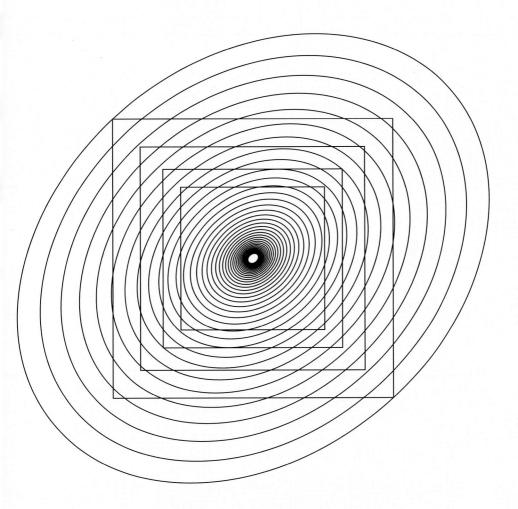

Little Big People

In reality, objects appear to be smaller the farther away we are from them. Naturally, the real size of the object doesn't change, only our perspective does. Yet in the world of optical illusions, a clever artist can turn perspective on its head. This drawing gives us the proper perspective cues. However, the couple in the distance looks bigger than the couple in the foreground. Is that really the case? To find out, measure both with a ruler.

There Was a Crooked Line... or Was There?

Don't get all bent out of shape if the lines on this illusion seem bent or crooked. They're actually straight!

Bodies Doubled

Sharing is often a virtue...or sometimes a virtual reality. Study this tangle of bodies and parts—drawn in a tradition long seen in Japanese, Chinese, and Indian graphic art—to see if you can figure out which parts belong to whom and how many full folks are really here.

Answer on page 94

Added Attraction

Our amazing eyes operate in a sort of stereo fashion, although at certain distances the two "channels" cross over. See for yourself by holding the bottom edge of this page up close and at eye level. You should see at least one, sometimes two, extra lines.

Crazy Legs

The top half of this hippo is fine, but the lower half is perplexing. See if you can figure out what's wrong with its legs—and why it would have a hard time charging.

Warning: Animals Lurking!

This may look like a bunch of scraggly trees and branches, but if you look more closely, you'll see something else. Hidden in this picture is a menagerie of animals. How many animals can you spot?

Skullduggery

Another popular, classic optical illusion—that's been drawn in countless variations—is to hide one (or more) image or images inside another. At first glance, you can easily see a skull with its gaping eye sockets and toothy grin. But look again at the sockets, and they become the reflection of a woman at the mirror of her vanity. Spooooky!

Wonder Women

This often-imitated illusion, which dates back to an anonymously illustrated German postcard from 1888, lets your brain "see" either an old woman or a young girl—depending on where your eyes start. For instance, the old woman's nose becomes the young girl's chin, and the woman's eye becomes the young girl's ear.

A Flag of a Different Color

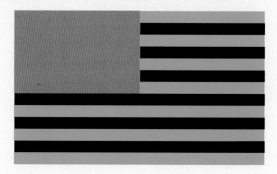

Stare at this flag for about 30 seconds. Try not to move your eyes. Then quickly look at a plain white wall or a blank piece of paper. You'll see Old Glory in her natural tri-colors. This is called an "afterimage," an illusion that occurs when our vision is over-stimulated. The image is more or less burned into your eyes, but in opposite colors, and reappears when you look at a blank space.

By George—Positively!

Gaze into George Washington's eyes for about 30 seconds, then quickly look at a plain white wall or a blank piece of paper. Your negative view of America's first president will instantly change, thanks to the afterimage effect.

Facin' the Music

Viewed from the left, you'll see a dark silhouette of a long-nosed jazzman wailing on his saxophone. But looking from the right, you can see a woman's face cast in deep shadow.

Split Personalities

From one perspective, this time-honored brainteaser seems to show the big eyes of someone in front of a lit candle in a holder. Seen from either the right or left, though, it can be two faces in profile, split by the candlestick.

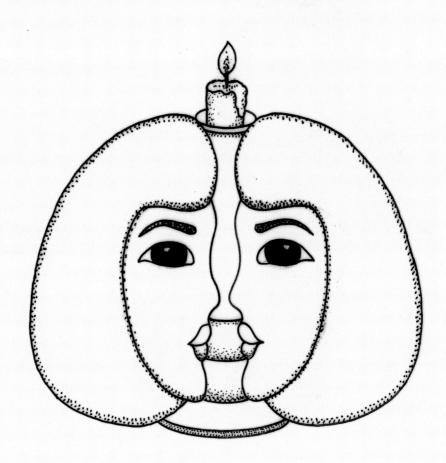

Ironical Twins

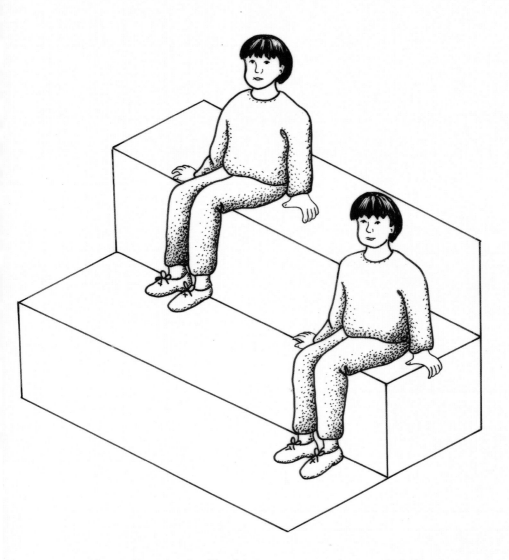

At first, these look-alike boys appear to be on their best behavior, but they're up to some visual mischief. The more you stare at the stairs they're sitting on, the less possible the picture becomes.

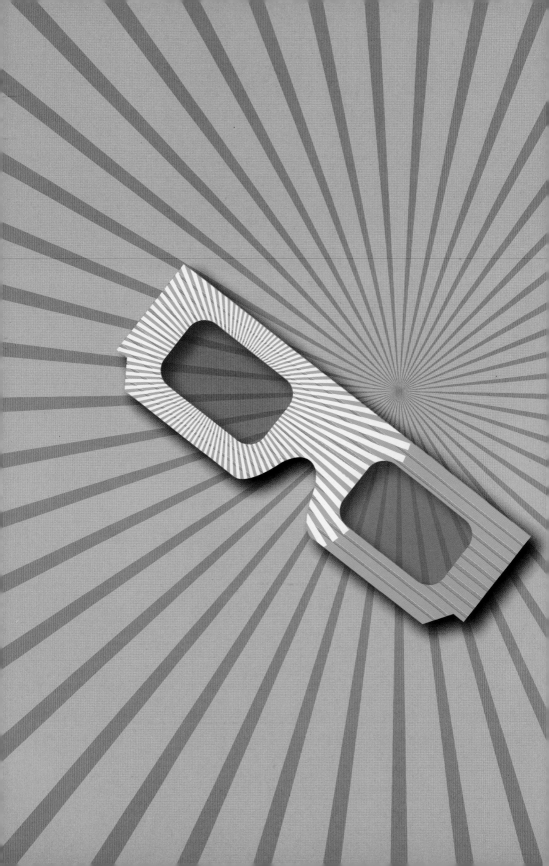

3-D Thrillers

Slip on those funny glasses and enter a wondrous dimension

Welcome to the wondrous world of three-dimensional imagery. This amazing effect—in which some objects seem to jump out at us while others recede—is less of an illusion and more a result of how our eyes work and some printing ingenuity. Slip on your 3-D glasses and check out pages 52—55.

Then explore the magical world of stereograms. What looks like an abstract jumble of color actually holds a computer-generated 3-D image hidden within. You don't need glasses. Just turn the book horizontally and stare at the dots on the top of each stereogram until you see a third dot, almost as if you're seeing double. Then focus intently on the center of the image. Relax your eyes, almost as if you're looking through it, not at it. Some people find it useful to hold the stereogram right up to their nose and then move it away without changing focus. It takes a little practice, but it's worth it.

Out on a Limb

Use your 3-D glasses.

Rock On!

Use your 3-D glasses.

Sting Operation

Use your 3-D glasses.

Open Wide!

Buried Treasure

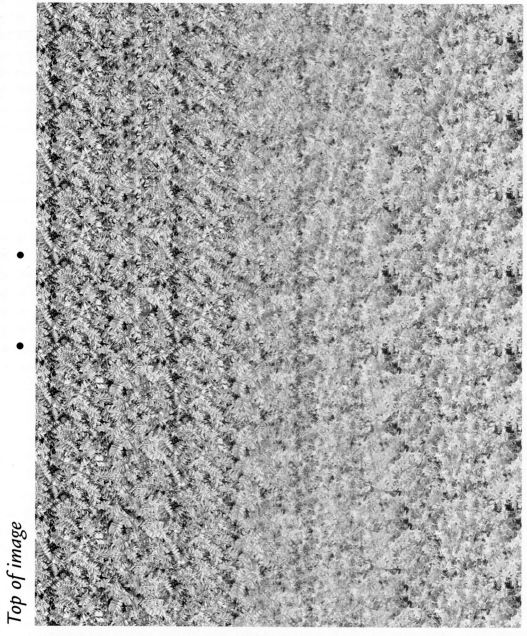

Top of image

Refer back to page 51 for instructions.

It Works...Really!

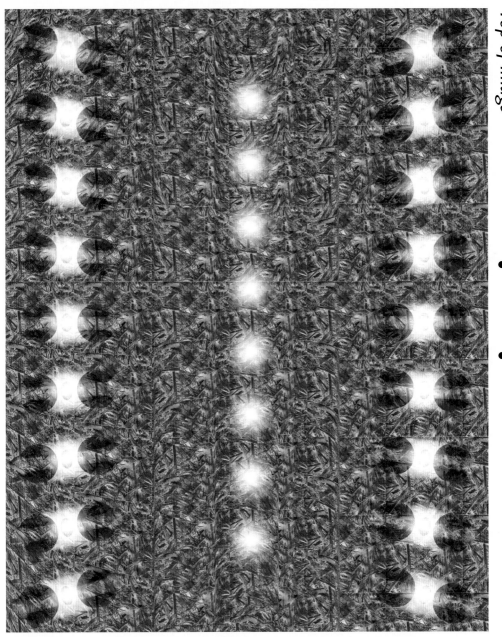

Answers on page 94

Flutter By

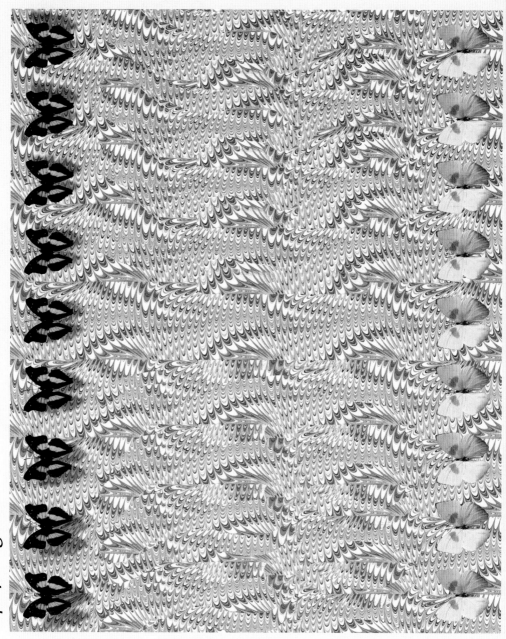

Dandy Lion

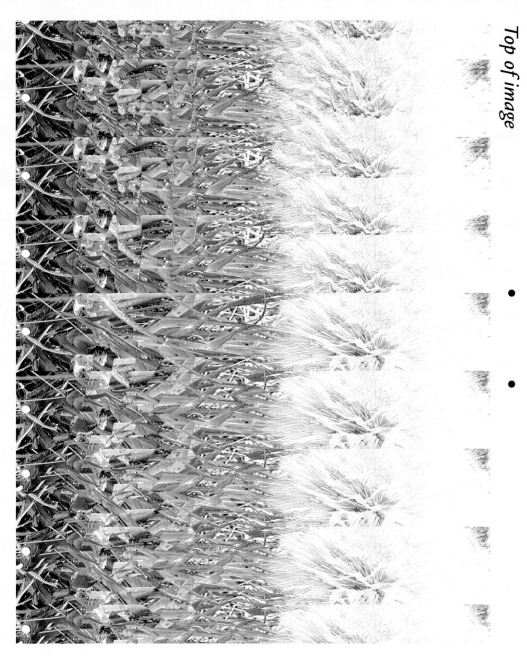

Top of image

Answers on page 94

Mirror, Mirror

Time for reflection

Let us reflect...on how mirror images can distort our ability to see things as they really are. First, you'll be a-mazed! Then you'll search for words to describe the trickery that is going on! Then you'll go half-crazy when the entire effect is revealed! And then finally...you'll probably do it all over again, because it's so much fun.

Maze Madness

So you think you know up from down? Back from forth? Here from there? Here's a test. Hold the mirror provided on the dotted lines next to the seemingly simple mazes on the next four pages. Looking at the mazes through the mirror,

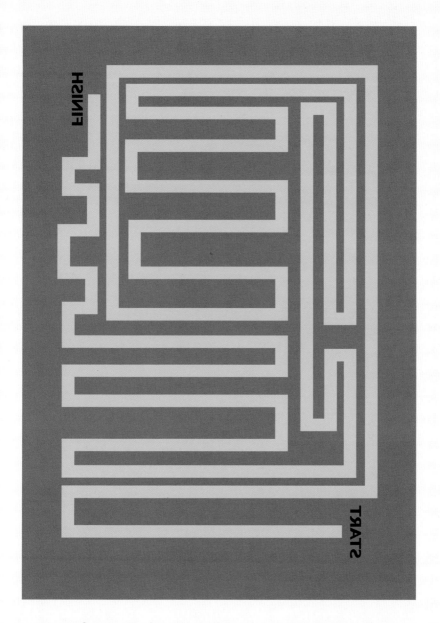

put your finger on the page where it says "START." Then
trace your way to "FINISH." You'll find in this case, the hand
is not quicker than the eye.

Finger Foolery

Try your luck guiding your finger through the mirror images of the lines in these mazes, too.

Answer on page 95

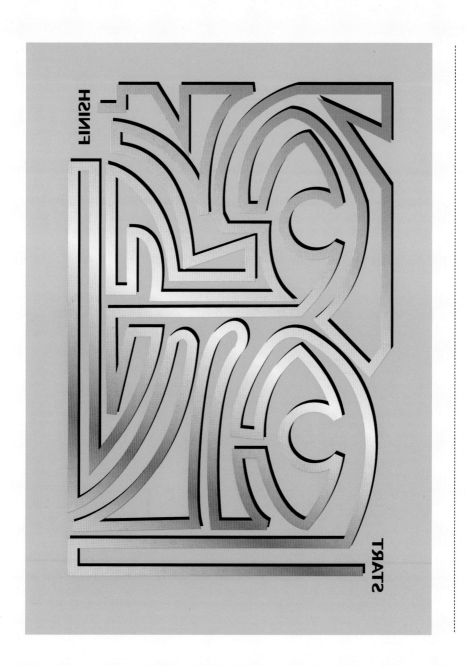

FINISH

START

Weird Wacky Words

DICE	ECHO
LODGE	BEAR
DECODE	DIED
WAX	WATER
CHOKE	COOKBOOK
POSE	PLATE
DECIDED	CHOICE
WHALE	YELLOW
HIDE	EXCEED
DIG	PEACH

Some of these words *are* weird, but not just because they are upside down. Hold your mirror next to each word. Looking in the mirror, see which of the words still reads correctly. Why can you read only the blue words and not the red ones? The answer is that the letters in the blue words are all symmetrical, unlike such letters as "g," "r," "k," and "p."

Test Your Half Wits

B
O
X

T
O
M
A
T
O

E
X
I
T

W
H
A
T

M
O
N
K
E
Y

W
O
W

M
O
U
T
H

C
A
T

Now hold the mirror on the dotted line that intersects each word, with the reflective side facing left. Why can you only read some of the words? This time it's the letters—when split in half—that are mirror images of themselves.

A Mirror Menagerie

Ready for more mirror magic? Use your mirror to complete the half-images on the next four pages. Hold the mirror along the dotted line on the edge of each picture. The mirror reverses the image, creating a totally symmetrical image where there once was an empty space.

Cat's Eye

Going Buggy

Just Clowning Around

Place your mirror on the dotted line to make this jester juggle eight balls!

Have a Ball

Soccer or baseball? You can play both, thanks to your mirror. Place your mirror on the dotted line to choose your sport!

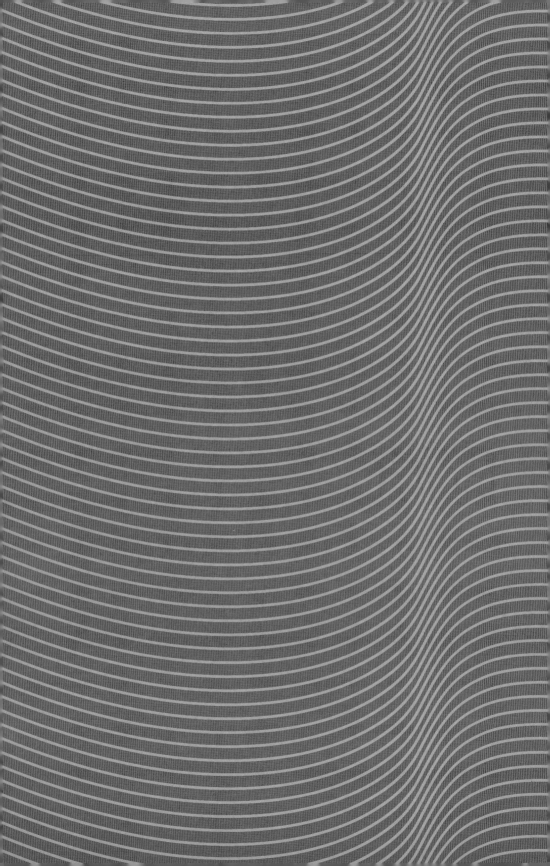

Special FX

*Make your own optical illusions
and see for yourself*

As we've seen with 3-D and mirror images, some optical illusions are revealed only with the assistance of visual helpers. Here are a few more crafty creations that require dipping back into your bag of trickery. Discover how combining two different patterns can generate an illusion of movement, and how crossing up our eyes' rods and cones can cause color chaos. Finally, take a deeper, super close-up view of the wonderful world of color using the colored films included in this kit.

The Moiré You See...
the Moiré You Like

Moiré is a French word that means "shimmering." The
effect occurs when you overlap two geometrically regular
patterns—such as these tightly aligned parallel lines—at slight

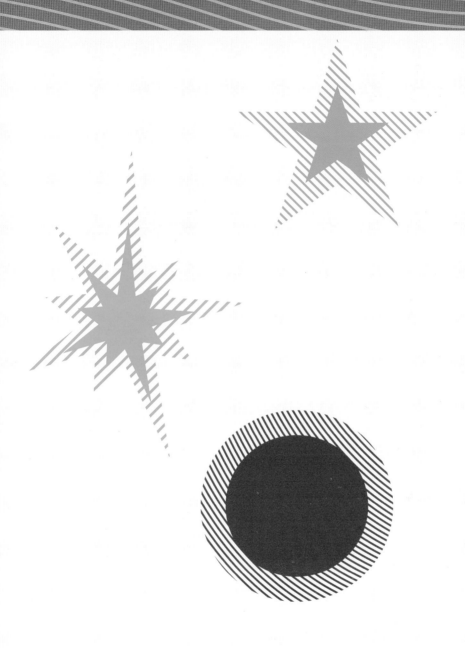

angles. Place your moiré film over each of the objects on these two pages. Move the film back and forth. Stand by for some spectacular special effects.

Good Vibrations

The patterns on these two pages can almost play tricks with your eyes alone. Combine them with your moiré film and they seem to vibrate and move.

Color Analyst

    Check out these blocks of color in a well-lit area. Now look at them in dim light. Can you see as many colors when the light is not as bright? The answer is no. It all has to do with your retinas. Each one features both rods and cones, which are cells that react to light and send messages to the brain, where the information is then processed.

Orange You Glad We Told You?

Look at this orange rectangle. Is it all the same shade?
Now, hold your finger vertically over the middle of the
rectangle. Why do there appear to be two different shades of
orange? Rods detect shades of gray. Cones detect colors. So in
dim light, the rods do most of the work, telling us that the
blocks on the previous page are duller than they really are. In
good light, the cones process the colors properly. Similarly,
when we look at the halved orange rectangle against a dark
background, it looks lighter than against the light background.

The Wonderful World of Color

The colorful images in this book are optical illusions in more ways than one. On the surface, they play tricks on your eyes and brain. Look under the surface though, and you'll see something else—another sort of illusion—going on. The color images in this book are printed using a series of tiny dots of four basic colors—yellow, magenta, cyan, and black. These colors can be combined to create all the other colors. Take the color photo of the cat above. If you look at the magnified inset photo, you can see how the tiny dots combine to create what appear to be solid colors. If you look at any printed four-color photo in a magazine or newspaper with a magnifying glass, you'll see the same phenomenon.

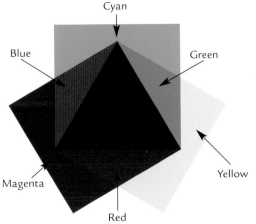

Cyan

Blue

Green

Magenta

Yellow

Red

It's also fun to play with color combinations. To see how the three primary colors can combine to create other colors, take the colored films included in this kit, and overlap them as shown.

Roses Are Red

The colors of this rose are a bit off, but see what happens when you place the yellow film over the petals and stem. Suddenly, the rose changes from pink to a rich red, and the leaves take on the correct green color. You can also experiment by placing the colored films over the color grid on page 78. See how the colors change.

Disc-o Fever

In this kit, you'll find a small disk with a bird pictured on one side and a cage on the other, plus two pieces of string. You can use them to make a "thaumatrope" (which means "turning marvel"). This is an illusion created by spinning the disk quickly to trick your eyes into seeing a single image incorporating the two illustrations on the disk. It works because your eyes are able to retain each image for about $\frac{1}{20}$ of a second after it has "disappeared," and your brain can't separate them. It's actually a simple form of animation.

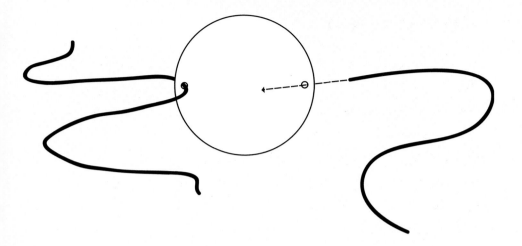

Begin by threading the string through the two holes on either side of the disk, as shown.

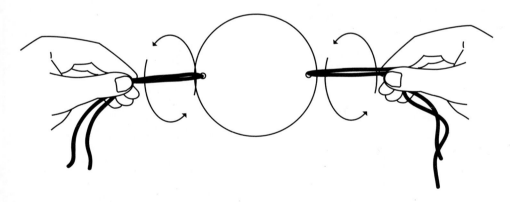

Now hold both strings with your fingers, and twist your fingers rapidly to make the disk flip around and around. Once you do, you'll see the bird magically "fly" into the cage!

Spin Your Wheels

In this visual trick, you're going to make a simple yet fascinating "phenakistoscope"—a rather long word that means "spindle viewer." As with the thaumatrope, this illusion relies on the "persistence of motion" principle that makes static images appear to move.

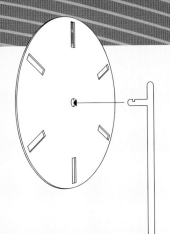

Set up your phenakistoscopes by using the two-sided slotted picture disks and the spinner stick included with this kit. Attach any of the disks to the stick, as shown in the illustration.

Position yourself in front of a mirror. Hold the disk at eye level, with the stick side facing you and the side with the images you want to animate facing the mirror.

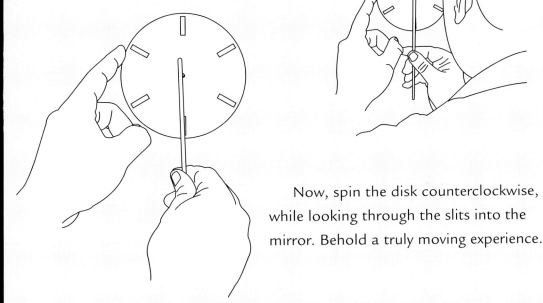

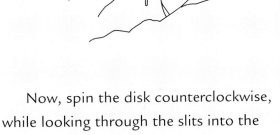

Now, spin the disk counterclockwise, while looking through the slits into the mirror. Behold a truly moving experience.

For a demonstration of simple animation, check out the page numbers in this book. When you flip the pages quickly, you'll see the wheel spin.

Eyes'll Be Seeing You

Get ready for an eerie eyeful of fun with a couple of innocent-looking animals. You're going to put some peepers on the pussycat and the owl. Begin by assembling the pictures, eye strips, and stands included with this book.

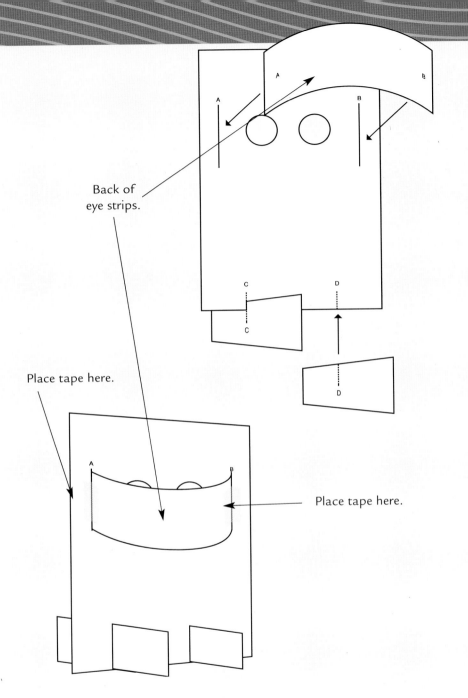

Back of eye strips.

Place tape here.

Place tape here.

As shown in the illustration above, insert tabs A, B, C, and D into their corresponding slits. Tape A and B as indicated. Then prop up the picture and walk back and forth in front of it. Watch as those magic eyes seem to follow you.

The Case of the Missing Finger

Here's a handy magic trick and optical illusion. You'll need the "Magic Box" component contained in this kit. Before long, you'll have your friends and family shaking their heads in puzzled amazement. In this trick, it will appear as if your finger disappears after you've put it in the box. How's it done? Like the cliché says, "It's all done with mirrors."

Mirror

Punch out the Magic Box piece from the card in this kit. Place it as shown, yellow side up.

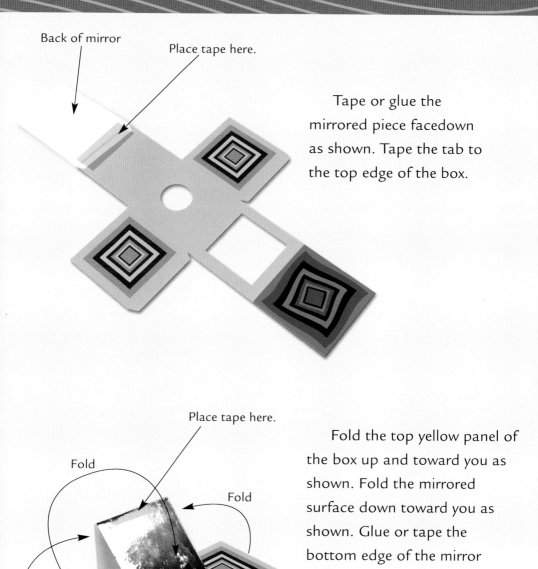

Back of mirror

Place tape here.

Tape or glue the mirrored piece facedown as shown. Tape the tab to the top edge of the box.

Place tape here.

Fold

Fold

Fold

Place tape here.

Fold the top yellow panel of the box up and toward you as shown. Fold the mirrored surface down toward you as shown. Glue or tape the bottom edge of the mirror along the dotted line. Fold the two side panels (yellow and red panels) up as shown.

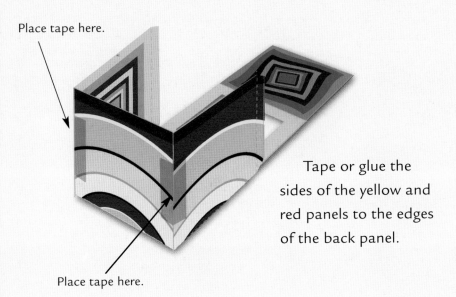

Place tape here.

Place tape here.

Tape or glue the sides of the yellow and red panels to the edges of the back panel.

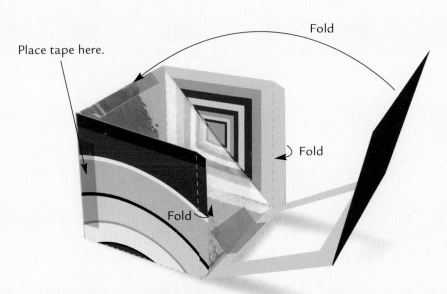

Place tape here.

Fold

Fold

Fold

Bring up the front panel so the blue square is on top and the window faces you.

Place tape here.

Place tape here.

Tape remaining edges
where indicated.

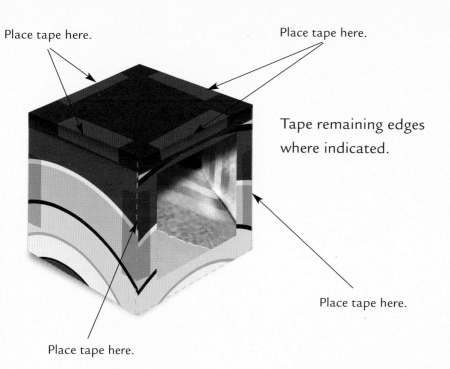

Place tape here.

Place tape here.

Turn the box over so the round
hole is now on top. Tell your friends
to watch your finger disappear as
you stick it into the hole.

The reason this trick works is
your finger is actually hidden behind
the mirror, while the mirror reflects the sides
of the box. The reflection of the pattern makes
it appear as if your finger has disappeared.

I Wanna Hole Your Hand

Here's a painless way to put a hole in your hand. Find an empty paper towel tube, or roll a sheet of paper into a tube shape. Hold the tube close to your right eye. Hold your left hand next to the tube, as shown in the illustration. Now with both eyes open, look at the tube and at your hand, focusing in the distance. Incredibly, it looks as if there's a hole through your palm!

The Floating Finger

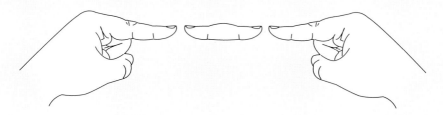

Now you're going to "grow" an 11th finger. Hold your two index fingers in front of your eyes so they are barely touching. Looking "through" your fingers, focus on something in the distance. An extra floating finger should mysteriously appear. Check out what happens when you move your fingers closer, then farther away from your eyes. The effect will grow on you!

Finger Food for Thought

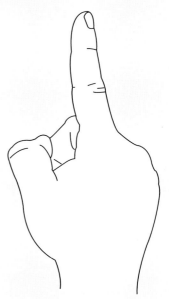

Here's a way to demonstrate your "binocular vision," which means that each eye sees the same object differently. Look at something in the distance. Hold your index finger at arm's length. Close one eye and notice where your finger appears. Now open that eye, close the other, and watch your finger jump. Do the same thing, but with your finger a few inches from your eyes, and it will jump even farther.

Answers

Page 28 Eye Exam
THIS IS HARD TO READ!

Page 31 Different Point of View
OPTICAL ILLUSIONS ARE COOL TO LOOK AT!

Page 41 Bodies Doubled
10 figures.

Page 56 Buried Treasure
See image A below.

Page 57 It Works...Really!
See image B below.

Page 58 Flutter By
See image C below.

Page 59 Dandy Lion
See image D below.

A
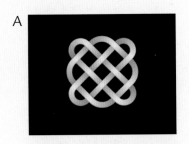

B
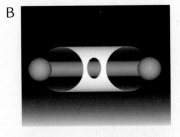

C
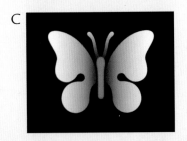

D

Page 64 **Finger Foolery**

Answers (Continued)

Text on Cover of Box
INCREDIBLE OPTICAL ILLUSIONS

Text on Inside Cover of Kit
THIS BOOK WILL BE FUN

Maze on Inside of Kit